OREGON II

OREGON II

PHOTOGRAPHY BY RAY ATKESON

TEXT BY ARCHIE SATTERFIELD

Left: Blossom of Oregon grape, state
flower of Oregon.

OREGON II

International Standard Book Number 0-912856-15-7
Library of Congress Catalog Number 74-75124
Copyright© 1974 by publisher • Charles H. Belding
Graphic Arts Center Publishing Co.
2000 N.W. Wilson • Portland, Oregon 97209 • 503/224-7777
Designer • Robert Reynolds
Printer • Graphic Arts Center
Binding • Lincoln & Allen
Printed in the United States of America
Fifth Printing

Wahkeena Springs emerging from forest
floor in the Cascade Range.

Kiwanda fishing dory heads toward beach near Pacific City. Right: Pacific breaker explodes as it meets the cliffs of Cape Kiwanda. In background, Haystack Rock. Following pages: View from Pilot Butte in Bend. Sunset silhouettes the high volcanic peaks of the Cascade Range.

Early autumn, aspen in the Upper Klamath Basin. Left: Remnants of a winter storm relax, permitting a peek at Mt. Hood. Following pages: Grove of aspen along shore of Upper Klamath Lake. In background, symmetrical cone of Mt. Harriman.

Gentle rain places crystal jewels of water in the clasp of lupine leaves. It is the most fragrant of western wildflowers growing in many areas of the Pacific Coast. Right: Fog envelops Cape Lookout State Park.

Imagine for a moment you have never been to Oregon; that you are living in the Midwest of 120 years ago. You keep hearing stories about the Oregon Country . . . a former mountain man comes through organizing a wagon train to the Willamette Valley. You listen to him, ask a few questions, like his answers, go home and, after supper, go out and stand on the porch. There are no snowcapped mountains in your line of vision. There are no blue lakes lined with evergreens. No silent forests from which a single tree can provide the lumber for a house. No fish-choked streams. In your interior vision, you already have picked out a place with meadows for hay and crops, trees for buildings and fences, a stream for water and irrigation if needed, and a mountain range for a backdrop.

You go back inside the house, take a deep breath and announce to your family: "We're going to take the trail to Oregon."

Today, with the population spreading across the magnificent landscape—a native was overheard saying, in all seriousness, that there are no ugly places in Oregon; some are just prettier than others—the state retains much of its unspoiled quality that attracted and kept the first white settlers.

While other states boast about the diversity of scenery within their boundaries, Oregonians don't have to make much of an issue of it. They are secure in the knowledge that they have mountains of all sizes, rivers of all depths, lakes in ample numbers, orchards, wheat farms, cattle ranches, deserts, rain forests, their fair share of ocean, and geology to boggle the mind.

Often, when entertaining friends or relatives they left behind back East, they are at loose ends where to take them first. The coast? The Columbia River Gorge? The Cascades? The high desert? A float trip on a river?

If they are coming by highway, you'd probably want them to take a leisurely trip up through Baker, La Grande and Pendleton in the high valley between the Blue and Wallowa Mountains. If they have enough time, you'd recommend a side trip up to Enterprise in the heart of the Wallowa Valley, the Valley claimed as the ancestral home by Chief Joseph, where the Nez Perce began their epic military campaign, a masterpiece of strategy that saved his people's lives while escaping from their beloved land.

Repeatedly, we hear visitors to the Wallowa Mountains say that they can easily understand why the Nez Perce fought so long to keep their land. With its vast lakes, rich valleys and open timber country, it is a land rich in natural bounty. True, the winters may be colder than other parts of the state, but that is an inconvenience

the Nez Perce—and present residents—are happy to tolerate.

Just as the Nez Perce were proud of the Appaloosa horses they raised, the ranchers of the northeastern part of the state take pride in the stock they raise. Some of the ranches specialize in purebred cattle and horses, and the life of a ranch-reared child is the envy of children who live in town.

The heart of the Wallowa region south of Enterprise is the rugged Eagle Cap Wilderness Area, high country crowned by eleven named mountains more than 9,400 feet high: Matterhorn (9,832 feet), Petes Peak (9,675 feet), Aneroid Mountain (9,702 feet), Sacajawea Peak (9,839 feet), Red Mountain (9,555 feet), East Peak (9,447 feet), Twin Peaks (9,463 & 9,673 feet), Chief Joseph (9,617 feet), Eagle Cap (9,595 feet) and Sentinel Peak (9,401 feet). Numerous streams course through the valleys between the granite peaks. At least 60 lakes, numerous hiking or horseback trails and dozens of abandoned mine shafts are found in the wilderness.

The state's northeastern boundary is one of the most spectacular areas of scenery in the Northwest. Here is found the Grand Canyon of the Snake River, the deepest gorge in North America. Remote, difficult of access, there are no broad highways leading into the area.

Often this far northeastern corner is ignored by those unaccustomed to straying from the main population areas of the Willamette Valley. But, in the Wallowas, one finds the scenery similar to the high country in the Rocky Mountain states. A drive through the Wallowas in the spring or autumn is the kind of pleasant experience one will remember for years to come. It is especially recommended for those who complain that the forests in the Cascade Range are too dense.

Another memorable experience, one that seldom grows tiresome for anyone, is cresting Deadman Pass (4,193 feet) heading to Pendleton from La Grande. The sight of those fertile valleys far below, with the Umatilla River flowing through, is still a thrill, as it must have been for those heading westward in wagon trains a century or more ago.

It is livestock country with cattle ranches, wheat farms and row crops around it. It is in the middle of some great fishing, hunting and riding country, and dude ranches dot the region.

Agriculture, or perhaps agronomy or agri-business would be more specific, is growing rapidly in the broad valley floor west and north of Pendleton. Land that once was consigned to rattlesnakes, jackrabbits and dust devils has become a major farm area for potatoes, melons, wheat and a variety of other crops. The secret is no secret at all, of course: it is water. By drilling deep wells, and in some cases pumping water from the Columbia River, the desert can become a garden in one growing season.

Those first emigrants who plodded along, day after day, behind their ox-drawn wagons across this empty space would have a genuine surprise if they were permitted a peek into the century ahead of their rigorous voyages.

There are deeper gorges in the world than the Columbia River Gorge, and there are longer ones with raging rapids and dozens of waterfalls. But the gorge of the Columbia is without question the most beautiful in our country and certainly the most accessible. On short hikes away from the highway, you can stop at frequent turnouts to look up and down the river, to watch towboats working in the slack-water pools behind the dams, and boats navigating the locks around the dams. See a sunset in the gorge, go on a hike late in the day and feel darkness descend in the forest while you walk beside a noisy stream.

The central portion of the gorge, where it cuts through the Cascades, is the most popular, but the entire length of it is what makes it such an exciting trip: from the sand and sagebrush and hot winds of the east to the cool, green central and western portion with sheer cliffs and waterfalls ranging from a trickle to a torrent. In fact, one could easily spend a week hiking up the trails from the highway that lead to waterfalls and spectacular scenes.

In the gorge, one can expect a variety of weather conditions, and almost be certain of a strong wind coursing up and down the corridor the river has created through the mountains. In the summer, the wind is often hot and dry; in the winter, cold and damp. Or, vice versa, depending on whether it comes down from the east or upriver from the sea. Fog is frequent, and in the winter a silver thaw can be expected sometime before spring arrives. These ice storms make for hazardous driving conditions, endanger crops and trees but create beautiful scenes for photographers, painters and others who enjoy nature on its own terms.

The river itself, in the gorge, is no longer a river but a series of man-made lakes behind hydroelectric dams. Gone, probably forever, are The Dalles (the stair-step rapids, not the charming town by the same name), the Cascades and perhaps the most photogenic spot on the entire Columbia River—Celilo Falls. There, for centuries, Indians speared and netted salmon as they jumped up the falls on their way upstream to spawn in tributaries of the river.

While these things are gone, along with the rushing water, the pleasure boaters enjoy the river much more now than when they had to portage around the falls and rapids. And sometimes, the still water has a beauty of its own, particularly early in the morning or late in the evening when the mountains and cliffs are reflected on its surface.

Most certainly the men who operate towboats on the river, pushing barges of petroleum products or grain, would prefer navigating the slack water rather than fast water. These men are keeping alive the tradition established during the big migratory push to the Oregon Country when flimsy, uncertain boats hauled people, cattle and wagons down the river toward the magical Willamette Valley, the crossroads where they could either head south into Oregon or north into what eventually became Washington.

Below Bonneville Dam, the last one downstream, the river's character changes again. From this point onward to the sea it is subject to the tidal action of the sea, mild and hardly perceptible at first, more pronounced as the river progresses westward. This is the Lower Columbia.

Its major tributaries are picked up below Bonneville Dam: the Willamette, Lewis, Cowlitz and finally the Lewis and Clark River. It becomes an inland sea with a salty tang to the air, flocks of sea gulls, a tidal action that can stop a tugboat in its wake. (Few towboats are used below Bonneville, except to pick up or deliver barges in the Portland-Vancouver area. Strangely, towboats push their loads, tugboats pull them.)

The character of the landscape changes dramatically below Bonneville, too. The Cascade Range gives way to foothills, then flat bottomland that is diked to keep the occasional flood in the river's channel. The population increases as the gorge gives way to the flatlands, and wilderness areas yield to farmlands and factories, to boat basins and wading and swimming beaches.

Below Portland the river becomes even broader with a series of islands, sloughs and false channels. Highways continue to follow it on both sides and small towns with picturesque names are spotted along it: Scappoose, Columbia City, St. Helens, Goble, Prescott, Rainier, Clatskanie, Brownsmead and Knappa.

After the river takes its final swing westward and heads directly for the Pacific Ocean, another commercial factor enters: the gillnetters. When the salmon are running, gillnet boats, many based on the last fifty miles of the river, go out during the shorter and shorter seasons to drift with the current on a slack tide, nets stretched outward at a right angle from the boat.

Inland from the river are the dairy farms, the forests

of the Coast Range, and the mint farms that distinguish the northwestern corner of Oregon. And at the river's estuary is an area of great historical significance: Astoria and the Lewis and Clark winter quarters at Fort Clatsop.

Situated upriver far enough to offer sheltered anchorage from the Columbia River Bar, Astoria figured prominently in the attempts to settle the Oregon Country. It was here that John Jacob Astor's ill-fated American Fur Company came and was conquered by geography, poor management, and the Indians. Yet, through the talent of Washington Irving in his novel, *Astoria*, the fur trading company has entered the mainstream of American literature. Irving's account of the Astor episode is highly imaginative, speculative and in many places wildly inaccurate, and for decades afterward the Oregon Country had a reputation of natural hostility it did not deserve. But the old adage that any publicity is good publicity applied. The American curiosity was aroused; the westward movement was on, the pioneers came.

There are probably thousands of residents in the Northwest who believe Astoria is on the coast, that breakers pound outside motel rooms and lull guests to sleep. And, although it is several miles inland, it usually is considered part of the famous Oregon Coast itinerary, just as the Astoria-Megler Bridge is generally referred to as being at the mouth of the Columbia.

True, waves do wash up on the banks of the river at Astoria and it is a seaport. Perhaps to argue with those who so believe is splitting hairs that do not need splitting. There is a limit to how accurate one must be, and Astorians don't seem to worry about it. If they don't, should anyone else?

South of Astoria is one of America's most popular historic sites; the Fort Clatsop National Memorial. Of all the American explorers, none have become greater heroes than Meriwether Lewis and William Clark, who left St. Louis in 1804, boated and walked to the mouth of the Columbia River and returned to St. Louis in 1806.

The explorers were not terribly impressed with their winter quarters at Fort Clatsop. It rained continually and they were never possessors of a surplus of meat. But while in Oregon, as while enroute, they conducted themselves well with Indians and were among the best ambassadors the United States ever sent West to meet and negotiate with the native Americans.

One-hundred and fifty years after the explorers left the rough-hewn fort to the Clatsop Indians, the original fort site was found by using archaelogical methods—digging carefully and sifting the dirt—until the original floor plans of the fort were discovered. A new fort, a replica, was built by the National Park Service and visi-

tors today may visit the fort and see how tiny the living spaces were that winter. Everything is there except the fleas and "pore meat" the explorers complained of constantly in their journals.

A fort of another kind lies due west of Fort Clatsop. Originally one of America's coastal defense posts, Fort Stevens has been turned into the most heavily used state park in the state's system. With miles and miles of surf and sand dunes, freshwater lakes within sight of the surf, low and dense timber for shelter from the storms that frequently rake the coast, the park has variety and comfort to offer visitors. It also is close enough to the fishing towns of Warrenton and Astoria for charter fishing outings, which account for the park's popularity.

People are always dividing the coast into sections, which is dictated mainly by access highways from the Willamette Valley and the larger towns at the terminus of those highways. Thus, we refer to the Seaside area, which includes Gearhart and Cannon Beach, Tolovana Park, Manzanita and so forth. Then there's the Tillamook area, Lincoln City and Newport. Other divisions include the Florence area; Coos Bay; Bandon and the southern coast. The latter includes Port Orford, Gold Beach and Brookings.

Obviously, by such generalized divisions, one cannot do justice to the variety of the coast. At first glance, all towns anywhere are similar. But you have to "stop and visit awhile" to learn that each town has its own personality, its own peculiarities and its own charm. They must be savored to be enjoyed.

While it is certainly true that tourism represents a major portion of most towns' income, there are many other industries represented. There are few towns on the western side of the Coast Range that do not have loggers as residents, those men who frequently leave home long before daylight and return after dark each day to work for the large timber companies who have vast land holdings back in the Coast Range. There also are commercial fishermen who cruise in and out of the river estuaries after salmon, albacore, tuna, crab and other gastronomical delights of the sea.

And there are the artists and writers who are attracted to places where nature is more evident than in cities, and where tourists have come to expect to find artwork for sale by the persons who created them.

When one thinks of rivers in Oregon, somewhere in the top three mentioned will be the Rogue, which winds through southwestern Oregon from its birthplace at Crater Lake to the Medford-Grants Pass area, swings north and then cuts back southwest toward the ocean through the Siskiyou National Forest. It is undoubtedly the most popular river to run in Oregon, and one of the major ones on the West Coast.

A particular favorite way to run the Rogue is from Wedderburn, near Gold Beach, upriver in the jet-powered mail and passenger boats. But the Rogue also is one of those man-sized rivers that is small enough—and rugged enough—to have its own personality. This, of course, means it is a challenge to those who like to take a canoe or kayak to a launch site, shove off and have at it.

There are numerous other rivers in Oregon with the same built-in challenge: The McKenzie River near Eugene, where, for many years, an annual white water parade was held as a test of boaters' skill and endurance. The McKenzie has become part of American craftsmanship via the distinctive dories built especially for use on it by sportsmen and river guides.

Over in the extreme southeast corner of the state is a small river that many lifelong residents have hardly heard of (Oregon tends to be that way: so many parts to it that it is difficult to see the whole). The Owyhee River flows northward from Idaho and near the Oregon-Nevada border through the small ranch town of Rome, picking up a few feeder streams before it reaches a dam near Adrian, then empties into the Snake near Nyssa.

For a short time each spring, at the height of the run-off, the Owyhee is a good river for canoes, kayakers and inflatable boat buffs. It winds through spectacular, barren canyons and offers enough rapids to keep the trip interesting.

The Deschutes, in north-central Oregon, is another favorite with both river-runners and fishermen, especially during the salmon-fly hatch in early summer and in the fall steelhead runs.

There are dozens of other rivers in the state that offer both excitement and relaxation for outdoorsmen, whether they work from the bank or go out among the boulders, backwashes and snags. Each has its own personality depending on how easily it floods, how the fishing is, what class rapids it offers, and how far from home.

If Oregon were a teeter-totter, its western end would be perpetually flat against the ground. The vast majority of its population is in that broad valley between the Cascade Range and the Coast Range that line the state north to south. Generally referred to as the Willamette Valley, the southern section from Cottage Grove south to the California border is not tied to the Willamette. The latter section is more tied to names of cities than a river: the Roseburg area, Grants Pass and Medford, although there are exceptions, such as the Valley of the Rogue and the Applegate Valley.

One of the more delightful places to visit in this southern valley is the historic town of Jacksonville, a former gold-rush town that has been turned into a living museum by its citizens.

Little has changed there so far as appearance goes. The grand old mansions built by those who struck it rich still stand, and the former county seat building, now the Jacksonville Museum, houses the collection of Peter Britt, an early settler there who was also an excellent photographer; the first, by the way, to photograph Crater Lake. During the final two weeks of August each year the Peter Britt Music Festival is held in Jacksonville's United States Hotel and gardens.

This also is Jesse Applegate country, one of Oregon's true pioneers, and to many, the most popular of Oregon's first residents. Applegate knew most of the mountain men—Jedediah Smith, David Jackson and William L. Sublette of the Rocky Mountain Fur Company among them—and through their stories and encouragement, Applegate struck out from his farm in Missouri to the Oregon Territory. He later wrote a book about his travels across the continent that today reads like an adventure novel. Applegate became one of the major political forces in Oregon, and his contributions are recognized by the town, river and valley named for him.

Only a few miles south is one of those paradoxes that confound festival directors: the Ashland Shakespearian Festival. When it was founded in 1935, some predicted it would not, it could not, be a success. Yet it is and has been for many years. Far from major population centers and in an area more noted for its farming and hunting and fishing than its cultural offerings, the Shakespearian festival now is a major part of American culture, and certainly a cornerstone of Oregon's cultural life. For an actor to have appeared at Ashland, or a director to have directed a play there, is an important addition to their credit list.

Since Interstate 5 bisected Oregon north to south, the Willamette Valley, so sought after by caravans of wagons, is still one of Oregon's beauty spots in spite of the growing population along the river.

The river isn't as accessible as one would expect because highways were built on the high ground, frequently out of sight of the river, to avoid floods. But there are numerous access roads leading off the old Highway 99 between Eugene and Portland, and where there are no bridges, there are small ferries that haul four to six cars across at a time.

For a number of years the Willamette was polluted, but state and federal regulations put an end to dumping untreated wastes into the river, and today it is again clear and clean. Frequently you can stand on the bank of a quiet pool and count each rock on the bottom, and a canoe drifting across the clear water looks almost as if it were floating in the air above the stream.

The cities along the Willamette have a people-oriented approach, and there is none of the uncontrolled-growth feeling to them. Eugene is a combination of lumbering and logging plus the University of Oregon. In the downtown area is a new shopping mall that is attractive both to residents and visitors because it is so open, airy and has children's playgrounds and a large free-form fountain that seems to invite one to sit and rest and gaze at the cascading water.

Eugene also is a bicyclist's paradise with miles and miles of paths through city and state parks in the area. One three-mile trail paved especially for bikes runs between Eugene and Springfield.

Only a short distance up the valley (the Willamette flows north, which leads to an "up is down and down is up" confusion to those accustomed to south-flowing rivers) is another charming small city, Corvallis. Taking its name from the Latin for "heart of the valley," it also is a college town with Oregon State University within its boundaries.

Its near neighbor, Albany, is noted for its Fourth of July Timber Carnival, and farther up the valley is Salem, the capital city. It is an old, charming city with broad streets lined with ancient trees, and is the home of Willamette University, founded in 1842 by the pioneer missionary, the Rev. Jason Lee.

Since Portland is a major West Coast seaport, it is often assumed by non-residents that it is a saltwater port. When they're told otherwise, they find it hard to believe that Portland is 100 miles from the ocean. But with its location, at the junction of the Willamette and Columbia Rivers, and with the rich agricultural land upstream on both rivers, Portland is ideally situated for commerce.

But people have not been forgotten. It is considered by the casual visitor as well as the long-term resident one of the most liveable cities in the world. One major requirement for a liveable city is that it offers an abundance of recreational possibilities, both within its corporate limits and only a short distance away. Consider what Portland offers before moving into its outlying areas:

Washington Park is one of the most wooded parks in a West Coast city. Anyone who has visited its nearby zoo is acquainted with the diminutive passenger trains that wind through the zoo on trestles and around hillsides, and through stands of timber as it takes you through both Washington Park and the Hoyt Arboretum, and up a steep hill with a great view of Portland.

Known as the city of parks to many, this city of trees and roses and open spaces has six major parks totaling 7,200 acres, with forests of hemlock, Douglas fir, western red cedar, native rhododendrons and azaleas.

Add to this the ice skating available throughout the year at Lloyd Center and other rinks—a spectators' sport as well as a participating one—and the boat cruises on the Willamette River and the gigantic Auditorium Forecourt fountain that is a series of waterfalls, there's seldom an excuse for anyone to bemoan the lack of something to see or do in Portland.

And that's just the beginning. Portland is close enough to the beaches and good fishing and floating rivers for its residents to go on day trips and get plenty of sun and exercise. Skiing is close by at Mount Hood, mountaineering almost in sight of downtown; bicycling, museums in the city and in smaller towns less than an hour away, bird watching on islands in the Columbia River, or just standing on the bank of either of the two big rivers and watching the floating traffic go by.

Portland is ideally situated for the active or those who enjoy watching the active people at work or play. It is not a sedentary city. An editor from New York City once remarked that back there people always seemed in a hurry to get somewhere else; in Portland, they didn't seem to want to go anywhere else.

From nearly any hill in Portland you can see the Cascade Range, or at least the king of Oregon's portion of the Cascades, Mount Hood. Mountains are beautiful to all, meaning something different to each of us. To a logger they represent his livelihood; to a fisherman a special lake or riffle; to a hiker that trail few other backpackers use; to an artist that special scene yet to be captured.

So the Cascades have many meanings to Oregonians. But all agree the mountains are one vast playground the year around. Numerous ski areas are available, and you're not considered a mountaineer until you're intimately familiar with Mount Hood's various routes and glaciers.

Six of the wilderness areas in Oregon are in the Cascades: Mountain Lakes to the northwest of Klamath Falls; Diamond Peak Wilderness to the north of Crater Lake; Three Sisters Wilderness between Eugene and Bend; Mount Washington Wilderness just north of Three Sisters; Mount Jefferson, actually part of Mount Washington but bisected by Highway 20; and Mount Hood, the most heavily used of them all.

Crater Lake is one of those natural oddities that continues to amaze each generation. Standing on the shore and looking out across the amazingly blue water and conical-shaped Wizard Island near the west shore, it is difficult to imagine the violence that occurred there some 6,600 years ago when it blew its own top off in a series of explosions that sent ash all over the Pacific Northwest and into Canada. Then, the mountain fell back inside itself, the crater filled with pure water and, after its discovery by the white man, became one of the must-see National Parks.

Farther north along the Pacific Crest Trail is Diamond Peak Wilderness, with the old volcano, Diamond Peak (8,744 feet), the lava peak of Mount Yoran (7,100) and an adjoining peak (7,138) as the centerpieces of the wilderness.

Three Sisters Wilderness surrounds the peaks that originally were called Faith, Hope and Charity, but later changed to the more geographically descript, but less colorful, names of North, Middle and South Sisters.

The wilderness area surrounds one of the greatest displays of volcano activity in the entire Cascade Range. All three of the Sisters—each in excess of 10,000 feet— plus Broken Top and Mount Bachelor are of volcanic origin. Scattered around the area are smaller cinder cones, lava tubes, pumice fields, dozens of lakes of all sizes and volcanic debris scattered at random.

There is both desolation and beauty in the Mount Washington Wilderness, where you find tortured lava flows and delicate flowers along the trails and beside craters where soil has managed to form since the last lava flowed perhaps as recently as 2,000 years ago.

In the view of many alpinists, the Jefferson Park in Mount Jefferson Wilderness is the loveliest stretch of alpine scenery in Oregon. This area is the most popular for hikers, and the 10,495-foot Mount Jefferson is nearly as popular as Mount Hood for climbers.

Mount Hood is divided almost in half by a wilderness area and proposals are being made frequently to extend the wilderness to include all of the peak. As it stands now, the southeastern portion of the mountain is in an open status, which includes the famous ski area around Timberline. At least 5,000 people climb the peak each summer on the south side from Timberline Lodge, taking as little as eight hours for the round trip. Even though it is Oregon's highest mountain at 11,245 feet, the ascent from the south is not particularly difficult for the experienced climber. Rougher trips are offered over the glaciers to the north, which become badly crevassed and rotten by mid or late summer.

For the less active, a popular trip from the Portland area is a triangular route to Government Camp and Timberline Lodge, which was built during the Works Progress Administration and completed in 1937. Since it was what has become known as a "make work" project, the talents of as many crafts and skills were utilized as possible—painters, wood-carvers, weavers, and stonecutters. As a result, it is something of a monument to craftsmanship of the era.

From the lodge, the route swings around the mountain and north to Hood River, then back down the Columbia River Highway to Portland.

Another popular way to see the area is along the 36-mile Timberline Trail that circles Mount Hood. The trip can be made in four or five days, and the Forest Service has spotted campsites at convenient locations along the way.

Of course, the grandpa of all hikes in Oregon—or the entire Pacific Northwest for that matter—is the Pacific Crest Trail. All 420 miles of it in Oregon. (This is subject to change due to alterations under way.) Obviously it is not a hike one would undertake on a two-week vacation, and only the few with an entire summer can "do" the entire trail in one season, unless they are interested in putting a lot of distance on their boots and not stopping for an occasional view of the scenery.

Unlike its neighboring coastal states, Oregon's landscape doesn't sink after it drops off the Cascade Range. Those who refer to Oregon's high desert are using the proper terminology. While California sinks well below sea level behind the Sierras, and Washington drops nearly to sea level, Oregon stays up there with the eagles. Bend is just over 3,600 feet; Burns, in the middle of the desert, is 4,100 feet, give or take a few feet, and Wagontire is 4,700 feet. It is definitely high, and it is definitely a desert, even though most books about the American Desert do not include it, perhaps under the East Coast impression that all of the state is inundated with tons of rain per square foot a year.

And the Oregon desert was—and still is—more Old West than the Old West itself. The range wars of Wyoming, the sheep of the other Rocky Mountain states, the gold rushes of Colorado and Arizona . . . all are part of our Saturday matinee and television culture. But students of Eastern Oregon are inclined to think that the high desert out "Old Wested" them all.

You can talk about a whole state and not mention a single person, and it usually won't be missed. But when it comes to parts of a state, a region as rich in history as the high desert, the conversation suffers if you leave personalities out. Eastern Oregon's high desert is not only a lot of landscape, it is a place where some fascinating men came in the early days of the white man's history there.

Peter French wasn't the first settler in what is now Harney County, but he was the first to attempt to own it. It was 1872 when French arrived with a herd of a

California rancher's cattle. French bought an outfit from a man who gave up on cattle in the desert, and ended up owning most of the grazing rights, but not the land itself, around Steens Mountain.

French did not build a big ranchhouse with a porch swing to sit in; he moved. He built, accumulated, experimented and became the owner of the best herd of beef cattle in this part of the country. He was a tycoon within five years of his arrival.

But his star fell nearly as fast as it rose. He married, but it was not a storybook marriage by any stretch of the imagination. His wife's father, French's partner, was murdered and when the dead man's tangled affairs were settled, French was nearly broke. He fought with the homesteaders. His wife divorced him and remarried. Lawsuits stacked up against him. Finally, almost mercifully it seemed, his misery was ended when a man named Ed Oliver murdered him.

Most of Pete French's ranch now is a wildlife refuge along Malheur Lake, and it still produces feed for cattle as well as for waterfowl that use the refuge.

When Hollywood was turning out its three-day films on the West, one subject underwent variation after variation: the cattle baron versus the sodbusters. Or, to be more accurate, those who needed thousands of acres for grazing to build up a good herd versus those who had good intentions, wanted a new place to set down their family roots, but who were unknowingly victimized by an East Coast government that did not understand the relationship between barren land, rainfall and row crops.

Usually these celluloid epics had Colorado or Wyoming as a setting with lots of men in black hats and black gloves, and "poor little men with their womenfolk and pack of kids." But Oregon was never mentioned in these films. In Hollywood, after the wagon trains reached the Columbia River and floated down to the Willamette River on flat-bottomed boats, everyone lived happily ever after.

That might have been true in some cases, but definitely not among those who came to Oregon after the Civil War to homestead the free land in the high desert. With the government's blessing and encouragement, they took over land that should never have been touched by the plow, turned it into a dust bowl, lost everything they owned, and moved on. Towns grew almost overnight, much like a gold-rush camp, only to be deserted in a year or two.

Gradually, the land has been reclaimed from the plow and returned to grazing land. Of course, there are the major exceptions, where the farmers have access to irrigation water or sink deep, deep wells to feed their crops.

We spoke earlier of the personalities that rugged country like the Oregon desert seems to either attract or develop. They're still there, but if you venture out into the desert in search of colorful characters, you'll be spotted immediately by those characters and very likely be subjected to either a long silence or a little special treatment. And you soon learn that most people live there because they want to, not because they don't know the way to Portland.

Much of the landscape of the desert is what writers refer to as tortured. There are vast lava beds scattered throughout the landscape east of the Cascades, and geological history is easily read because the erosion has not been hastened by an excess of water. As you wander across the southeastern corner of the state, it is difficult to imagine the forces at work that caused the landscape to assume the rugged beauty it has today. Instead of volcanic eruptions, creeping molten lava and steam vents, today there is only an intense silence.

But the lava did indeed flow; more than 5,000 feet deep in places as it sought out the low ground and filled the canyons with liquid stone. One of the most dramatic examples of this volcanic activity as recent as 500 years ago is the area northwest of Jordan Valley called the Jordan Craters. Here several volcanic cones surround one large one, all dark in color with clinkers tinted with blue, gray, green, brown and purple.

Near Rome are the stunning Walls of Rome, the high, carved sides of a dry tributary of the Owyhee River that stretch about a mile along the canyon.

Malheur Cave, near Princeton, stretches back into the lava about half a mile, making it one of the longer of the lava tubes that are found along the slopes of the Cascade Range. The cave is easily accessible and the walking is relatively safe because there are no passages leading off the main route to get lost in.

Obviously, this part of the state is a haven for rockhounds, and families come from all over the West to poke around the lava country for agates, jasper, petrified wood and thunder eggs.

A favorite spot for photographers is the 184,000-acre Malheur National Wildlife Refuge south of Burns. Sandhill cranes and trumpeter swans are among the 230-odd species that have been spotted in the refuge.

It must be emphasized that photographs and descriptions of a place—even as varied as Oregon—can at best give one a visual and verbal inventory of the state's natural beauty. Natural beauty alone is not sufficient to make a place inhabitable. If that were the only criteria, some heavily populated parts of this country would be vacated rapidly, or would never have been settled at all. And a place as beautiful as Oregon would be filled with people, like Holland or Japan.

Among other qualities required for a decent place to live and visit—even beyond the settlers' required good land, trees and water—one of the most important is an attitude toward life in general and one's home in particular. That attitude becomes part of the state's culture, and the early arrivals such as Jesse Applegate and Dr. John McLoughlin of the Hudson's Bay Company post at Fort Vancouver did much to establish the friendly, neighborly, helpful spirit that continues to this day.

Applegate, mentioned earlier for his literary abilities, was known by his contemporaries as the "Sage of Yoncalla." A homely man, he never permitted a photograph taken of himself during his life, and an artist's version of his profile made after death supports Applegate's opinion of his looks. But there was a Lincolnesque quality to the man, and he had the privilege of turning down an offer by President Lincoln to become governor of the Oregon Territory.

Applegate was a leader, an idealist, a prime force in the move to wrest the Oregon Country from English domination. He was also something of a legend in pathfinding. The Applegate Trail was laid out toward the end of the mass migration to the West Coast. It was one of the safest trails to Oregon, and one with the best conditions for travel. It split off the Old Oregon Trail in Idaho where the trail crossed the Raft River, between Pocatello and Twin Falls. From there, it swung south to miss the Snake and Columbia Rivers (where the Applegates lost three persons during their initial trip out), went south into Nevada through Wells, Winnemucca, Humboldt and back northwest into the tip of California at Surprise Valley, Tule Lake and crossed into Oregon near where Ashland is today, then went up the Willamette Valley.

He was instrumental in getting the Hudson's Bay Company to accept the measures of the provisional government of Oregon, which in turn led to the dual government of Oregon—the United States and Great Britain—which then developed into the Oregon Territory and eventually into statehood.

But Applegate's greatest contribution to the Oregon Country was an attitude of responsibility and generosity. He was the patriarch of a large family and owned a vast farm. He was noted for his hospitality, and his name became synonymous with the new land of the Northwest. He represented stability and intelligence.

Dr. McLoughlin's contribution was something of the same order, but with a major difference. He was an Englishman working for the English-owned Hudson's Bay Company, and part of his job, at least in theory, was to protect the fur-rich Pacific Northwest from American encroachment. So long as the HBC had at least token control of the vast Columbia River watershed, his employers would be happy.

Settlers, who first trickled, then flooded in from the existing United States, found him humane, helpful and not as imposing as one would expect the factor of a fur post for a foreign power to be. It was his kindness and generosity that gave many newcomers a fresh start in a strange land, and gave them an attitude of cooperation from the moment of their arrival.

These are only two examples of what made Oregon so attractive to newcomers. There are many instances, such as when the Applegate Trail users came into the plush, green Willamette Valley and found established farms with open gates and helpful owners. Most records—letters and diaries—from the period bear out the contention that, of all the goals of emigrants during the westward movement, the Oregon Country came closest to matching up with the expectations of those who sought a new land and a new life. And it is a feeling that still exists today.

So . . . imagine, for a moment, what kind of place you'd best like to live. Would it be near good fishing and boating waters? Would it be near trails that lead into solitude and natural beauty? Would it be in or near a city with a major mountain range as a backdrop and with a clean river flowing through its center? Would you like to be near a desert where you can see pronghorn antelopes and, if you're lucky, a herd of wild horses? Would you require a coastline that has no parallel anywhere on the continent, and also most of it be in public ownership?

And do your requirements include a mild climate, but not so mild that the seasons never change and the leaves never turn colors?

It is to Oregonians' credit that most of them do not feel compelled to brag about these conditions. When you have the good life, and Oregon offers it, there is no need to brag, just as there is no need to brag about having a good marriage or healthy, intelligent children. Rather, one tends to quietly enjoy these things. Otherwise, there is always the superstitious fear that by talking too much about something pleasant, its continuation might be endangered.

Unless, of course, it is simply a statement of fact. And one fact is as clear as a Cascade stream: Oregon is a great place to live.

Succor Creek Canyon State Park, midway between Jordan Valley and Ontario.

Example of determination to survive on the high desert in Lake County. Right: Spectacular spires in Leslie Gulch. Following pages: Brilliant sunset streaks across one of the countless lakes in Warner Valley.

Mann Lake Ranch at base of snow-capped
Steens Mountain. Right: Young antelope
in Malheur National Wildlife Refuge.

Avocets in Summer Lake State Game Refuge. Right: South Sister in Oregon's Cascade Range reflected in the crystal clear water of Sparks Lake. In foreground, columbine and other wild flowers bloom on small lava island just offshore.

Towering pinnacles dominate Leslie Gulch near Owyhee Lake. Right: Dramatic view of Hells Canyon of the Snake River. It is a thousand feet deeper than the Grand Canyon of the Colorado River.

Cattle grazing in the John Day Valley amidst seasonal colored cottonwood trees. In background, Strawberry Mountain sprinkled with the first snow of autumn. Right: Cattails in the John Day Valley.

Milk vetch on the summit of Mt. Emily in the Blue Mountains. Right: Aspen foliage identified with autumn's brilliant colors along the shore of Klamath Lake. Following pages: Sunset silhouettes birds in flight over Klamath Basin.

Youngs River Falls in northwest area of the Coast Range. Right: Sunlit vine maple at edge of mountain lake in Cascade Range. Following pages: Stonecrop on moss-covered rock in Columbia River Gorge.

Graceful maidenhair fern along edge of mountain stream in the Cascade Range. Right: Balsam root carpets the foothills of the Cascade Range overlooking Hood River Valley. In background, Mt. Hood.

Harvesttime foliage, Silver Falls State Park in foothills of the Cascade Range. Right: Icy water of the McKenzie spills down the slope of the Cascade Range near the headwaters of the river.

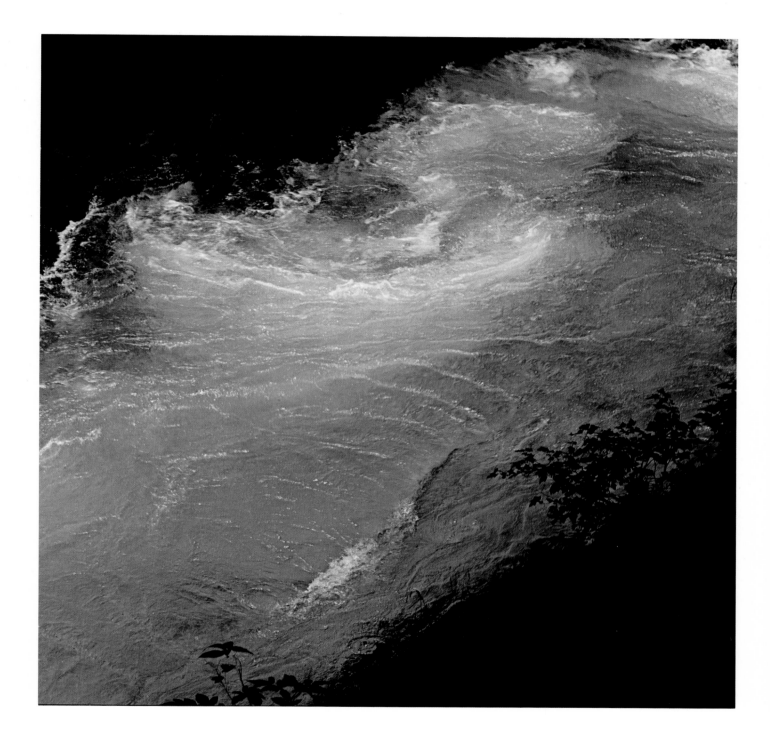

Club moss draped on maple tree depicts heavy rainfall on west slope of Coast Range. Right: Heceta Head light flashes its warning from site overlooking Devils Elbow State Park.

Salmon River Estuary from flower-sprinkled slopes of Cascade Head. Right: Sunset highlights rocky cliff at Cape Kiwanda along the coastal shore.

Cape Lookout State Park along the northern coast. Left: Roots of old tree bared by wave action near Cape Meares.

55

Graceful gulls at base of Cape Kiwanda.
Right: Rugged headlands on the central
coast.

56

Cormorants find nesting places in precarious spots on steep cliffs and ledges along the Oregon Coast. Right: Oregon Dunes National Recreation Area. Following pages: View from Tillamook Head, ground fog blankets coves and headlands.

Picturesque barn in foothills of Coast Range. Right: Long-standing, moss-covered maple heralds the coming of spring along shore of Alsea River in the Coast Range.

62

Historic home in Jacksonville. Left: North Umpqua River tumbles through a forest corridor in the southern Cascade Range.

Full-blooming pear trees in a Rogue River Valley orchard signal a bumper crop. Right: Lush pears in orchard near Medford.

Paradise Lost Room in Oregon Caves
National Monument. Stalactites descend
and stalagmites rise. Left: Boating party on
Rogue River at Horse Shoe Bend.

Wild rhododendron, (clockwise from upper left) wild iris, pink lamb's tongue, trillium. Right: Dahlia farm near Canby.

Sahalie Falls near headwaters of McKenzie River in the Cascade Range. Right: Indian summer along the Willamette River.

Timber grove on Tualatin Valley farm. Right: October colored foliage lends contrast to Lower South Falls in Silver Falls State Park. Twelve waterfalls are encompassed in this beautiful park in the western foothills of the Cascade Range. Following pages: Glorious sunrise tints fog shrouded Willamette Valley.

Wizard Island appears to float on surface of Crater Lake enveloped with blanket of snow. Left: Animal tracks in Cascade Range.

Pinnacles of the Phantom Ship create a rugged impression on the seldom-photographed surface of Crater Lake. Right: Spring in alpine meadow on crest of the Cascade Range.

View from crater of Lava Butte. Black Butte and Mt. Jefferson tower high into sunset haze that drapes the central Cascade Range. In foreground, pine tree, which grows abundantly in the eastern foothills. Left: Tumalo Falls spills over a high lava wall near Bend.

Five-mile-long Diamond Lake nestled between two major volcanic peaks on the crest of the Cascade Range. In foreground, Mt. Thielsen; in distance, snow-draped Mt. Bailey. Right: Gnarled snag on the crest of the Cascade Range in Three Sisters Wilderness represents centuries of battle with the elements.

Mt. Bachelor in the central Cascade Range, a popular winter playground. Left: Autumn sunlight sparkles on surface of Cascade mountain lake. Following pages: Vine maple leaves at their turning, rim shore of headwaters of McKenzie River on crest of the Cascade Range.

Shooting star, (clockwise from upper left) columbine, balsam root, yellow lamb's tongue. Right: Frigid winter weather creates spectacular formation at base of Horsetail Falls on Columbia River Highway. Following pages: Conifers thickly encrusted with ice and snow on slopes of Mt. Hood.

Morning sun illuminates the snow-crowned cone of Mt. Hood. Left: Mountaineers explore spectacular beauty of Eliot Glacier on Mt. Hood.

Phacelia Lineoris seems to adapt well to the semi-arid desert area near the Crooked River. Right: Sand dunes above the Columbia River near The Dalles.

Fort Rock, circular crater of ancient volcano in Lake County. Left: Indian paintbrush creates unusual contrast in field of sagebrush.

Cathedral Rock bares its colorful tiers above the John Day River in Fossil Bed National Monument. Right: After years of striving for survival, this weather-bleached pine remains upright in the Lava Butte area of central Oregon.

Dwarf mimulus carpets the floor of volcanic pumice where it spreads abundantly in this semi-arid climate. Left: The Crooked River in Smith Rocks State Park. Following pages: Painted Hills State Park near Mitchell.

Sunlit larch trees create interesting contrast in pine forest of Blue Mountains at Dixie Summit. Right: Late afternoon shadows across the John Day Valley at base of Strawberry Mountain. Following pages: Field of stubble at base of Blue Mountains in early winter.

Anthony Lakes ski area on crest of Blue Mountain Range. Right: Bronc rider at Pendleton Roundup. (clockwise from upper left) Elkhorn Ridge in the Blue Mountain Range, abandoned ranch building in high desert near Mitchell, cattle feeding on stubble of wheat.

Field of maturing wheat in Umatilla County. Right: Frost-encrusted shrubs on floor of Powder River Valley near Baker.

Absence of snow exposes the mountain crags and verdant meadows of the Wallowa Mountains. This area may be reached only by foot or horseback. Right: Looking east from Mt. Emily across the Grand Ronde Valley.

Remnants of volcanic slopes rise from floor of the Imnaha River Canyon. Right: Multi-hued lichen on the face of a lava cliff.

Countless rapids, deep gorges and colorful buttes make the Owyhee River one of the most exciting in the West. Right: Cattle grazing at the base of the Steens Mountain in Harney County. Following pages: Late afternoon sun highlights the golden grain fields in Wasco County.

Spectacular panorama of enormous dry lake bed in the heart of the Alvord Desert. Right: Lichen-covered lava creates interesting pattern on the volcanic rimrock in Harney County. Following pages: Late afternoon sun defines the alpine slopes of Mt. Ashland.

Dearth of snow exposes crags and glacier-clad slopes of Mt. Jefferson. In foreground, Bays Lake. Left: Remote lakes dot the Mountain Lakes Wilderness Area in the southern Cascade Range. In background, Mt. McLoughlin.

Conifers heavily laden with the mark of winter on the slopes of Mt. Bachelor. Right: Sunlit branch of larch tree denotes the advent of winter. The needles of this tree (often called tamarack) turn to gold in autumn and, then fall to the ground.

View from above Horsetail Falls captures a portion of the magnificent Columbia River Gorge. Left: Thin veil of cirrostratus clouds of tiny ice crystals creates halo around the sun indicating approaching foul weather.

Springtime in the Hood River Valley. Right: Necktie Falls on Wahkeena Creek in Mt. Hood National Forest.

Brilliant splash of color defines vine maple
on a mountainside near the McKenzie Pass.
Left: Rarely-photographed water ouzel
feeding its young in moss-covered nest at
edge of waterfall in the Cascade Range.
Following pages: The Tualatin Valley on a
summer day. In the distance, peaks of Mt.
St. Helens and Mt. Adams are visible.

Field of red clover carpets rich farmland in Willamette Valley. Right: Billowing fog blankets the Tualatin Valley seen from Council Crest Park in Portland. Following pages: The City of Portland and Mt. Hood at twilight.

Freezing winter temperatures make their mark in the Columbia River Gorge. Right: Clackamas River rushes through forest corridor in the Cascade Range near Estacada.

142

Peace rose developed by French hybridist
Meilland has been a favorite with American
rose fanciers since its introduction several
years ago. Left: Wild rhododendron in the
Kalmiopsis Wilderness area of the Siskiyou
Mountains.

Autumn colors abound along the Eagle Creek trail in Mt. Hood National Forest. Right: Covered bridge in Willamette Valley near Scio. (clockwise from upper left) Deady Hall, University of Oregon. Memorial Union Building, Oregon State University. State Capitol Building, Salem, Oregon.

Field of daffodils in the Willamette Valley. Right: Jewell Wildlife Meadows have been set aside by the Oregon Game Commission for the benefit of elk, deer and other wild animals in the Coast Range.

Sun highlights ships at anchor in Columbia River near Astoria. In background, Tongue Point. Right: Frost responsible for delicate pattern in holly orchard near Portland.

Red Delicious apples ready for harvest in Hood River Valley orchard. Right: Multnomah Falls drops 620 feet from Cascade Mountain rim to edge of U.S. Interstate 80N.

Yellow violets in the western foothills of the Cascade Range. Right: Proxy Falls just inside Three Sisters Wilderness in McKenzie River Area of Cascade Range.

Sheep graze peacefully on a farm in the central Willamette Valley. Right: Willamette River as it leaves the foothills of the Cascade Range.

The Willamette River Valley marked with lush farms and groves of evergreens. In foreground, raft of logs destined for nearby mill. On the horizon, 11,245 foot Mt. Hood. Right: Roaring Creek pours down the slopes of the Cascade Range.

Oak tree dominates a grassy hilltop in the
Tualatin Valley. Left: Moss-covered maple
screens the view of Munson Creek Falls in
Tillamook County.

Interstate Bridge spans the Columbia River between Astoria and north to the State of Washington. Right: Early morning sun silhouettes weatherworn piling along the shore of Tillamook Bay.

Cattle graze in pasture near Tillamook, the cheese capital of the West. Right: Veil of chilling fog hovers over the Tillamook River in early morning.

Weatherworn tree creates unusual contrast along the Pacific shore near Devils Churn State Park. Left: Steelhead fishermen accepting early morning mist on Siuslaw River in tidewater. Following pages: Sea gulls on the sands of Cannon Beach. In background, Haystack Rock and The Needles tower above the Pacific surf.

Oregon Sand Dunes National Recreation Area bordering the Oregon Coast Highway. Right: Sea Foam whipped up by a storm at sea, comes ashore at Fogarty Creek State Park. Following pages: Rain forest along Cascade Head trail near Neskowin.

170

Surf and foam spilling over shoreline table in Cape Kiwanda State Park. Right: Unusual pattern etched on sandstone in Seal Rock State Park.

174

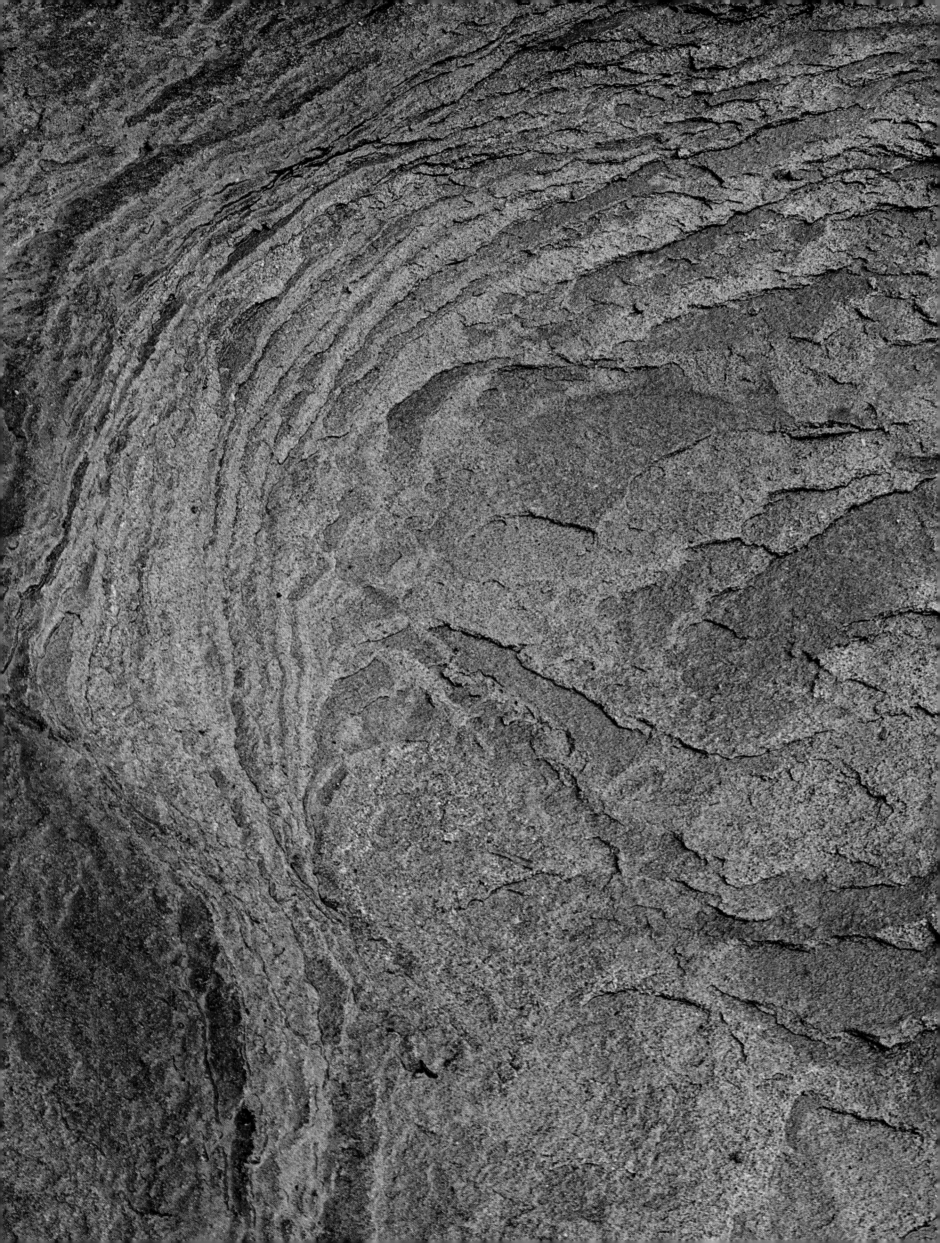

Lava flow from South Sister at edge of Green Lakes in the heart of the Three Sisters Wilderness. Right: Hole in Ground approximately 500 feet deep, result of abrupt volcanic explosion near Fort Rock.

East and Paulina Lakes nestle on the forested floor of the ancient Newberry Crater east of the Cascade Range. Right: State highway 204 swings down from the Blue Mountains into grain fields of Umatilla County near Weston.

Snow-crested ridges of Eagle Cap Wilderness Area tower above deep, forested canyons in the Wallowa Mountains. View from Mt. Howard reached by cable car. Right: Sheep grazing in Powder River Valley at base of the Blue Mountain Range.

Arid desert prevailed as sagebrush lost the fight for survival near Burns. In foreground, spring-blooming phlox. Right: Wild horses thunder across the high desert in Lake County. Over 6,000 roam this southeast area. Following pages: Morning sun delivers clear identity to crest of Steens Mountain Range under a spectacular cloud formation.

Old barn represents a special way of life in the Powder River Valley near Baker. Right: Clusters of lichen on sheer wall in Jordan Craters area.

Acres of blooming chives growing in the fertile Treasure Valley area near Ontario. Right: Wildflowers abut a forest road in the foothills of the Wallowa Mountains above Pine Valley.

Peas and grain adapt to the fertile earth below the Blue Mountains in Umatilla County. Right: Winter sunlight streaks across the icy surface of Klamath Lake.